W9-CIH-708

The War of 1812

Heroes of a Great Canadian Victory

by Jennifer Crump

As always, to Alex, Laura, Emily, Alexandria, Kathleen, and Danielle for their unwavering support.

PUBLISHED BY ALTITUDE PUBLISHING CANADA LTD.
1500 Railway Avenue, Canmore, Alberta T1W 1P6
www.altitudepublishing.com
www.amazingstories.ca
1-800-957-6888

Based on a book with the same title
by Jennifer Crump, first published in 2003.

Extreme care has been taken to ensure that all information presented
in this book is accurate and up-to-date. Neither the author nor
nor the publisher can be held responsible for any errors.

Publisher	Stephen Hutchings
Associate Publisher	Kara Turner
Junior Edition Series Editor	Linda Aspen-Baxter
Layout	Zoe Howes

We acknowledge the financial support of the Government
of Canada through the Book Publishing Industry Development
Program (BPIDP) for our publishing activities.

Altitude GreenTree Program
Altitude Publishing will plant twice as many trees as were used
in the manufacturing of this product.

Library and Archives Canada Cataloguing in Publication Data

ISBN 10: 1-55439-711-1
ISBN 13: 978-1-55439-711-2

Amazing Stories® is a registered trademark of Altitude Publishing Canada Ltd.

Printed and bound in Canada by Friesens
2 4 6 8 9 7 5 3 1

Note to readers
Words in **bold** are defined in the glossary at the back of the book

Contents

War of 1812 Chronology

Battle of Tippecanoe	November 7, 1811
U.S. Declaration of War	June 19, 1812
Capture of the Cuyahoga Packet	June 21, 1812
Hull occupies Sandwich	July 12, 1812
Fort Michilimackinac taken	July 17, 1812
Battle of Brownstown	August 5, 1812
Capture of Fort Detroit	August 16, 1812
Battle of Queenston Heights	October 13, 1812
Battle of La Colle	November 27, 1812
The River Raisin Massacre	January 19, 1813
Battle of Stoney Creek	June 6, 1813
Battle of Beaver Dams	June 24, 1813
Battle of Lake Erie	September 10, 1813
Battle of the Thames (Moraviantown)	October 5, 1813
Battle of Chateauguay	October 25, 1813
Battle of Chrysler's Farms	November 11, 1813
Burning of Newark	December 10, 1813
Burning of the U.S. Niagara begins	December 20, 1813
Battle at Chippewa	July 5, 1814
Battle of Lundy's Lane	July 25, 1814
Battle of Fort Erie	August 15, 1814
Washington burns	August 24, 1814
Treaty of Ghent	December 24, 1814
Battle of New Orleans	January 8, 1815

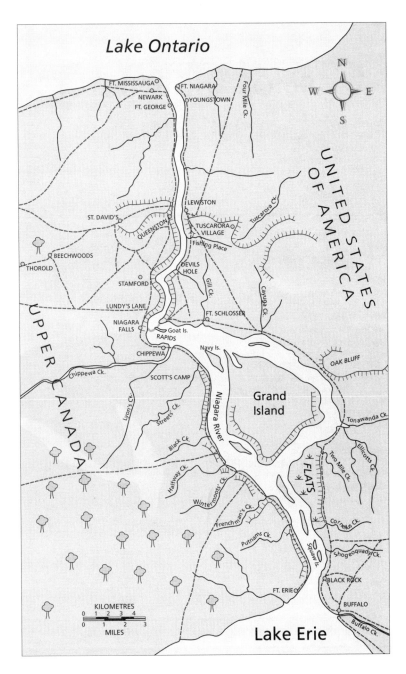

The Niagara Region in 1812

Cast of Characters

Americans
Lieutenant Colonel Charles Boerstler
Cyrenius Chapin
General Wade Hampton
Lieutenant Porter Hanks
Brigadier General William Henry Harrison
Brigadier General William Hull
Brigadier General George McClure
Colonel Winfield Scott
General Stephan Van Renasselaer
Major General James Wilkinson
Joseph Willcocks (Canadian who sided with the Americans)

British
Lieutenant-Colonel Cecil Bishop
Major General Isaac Brock
William "Tiger" Dunlop
Lieutenant James Fitzgibbon
Lieutenant Colonel John Harvey
Lieutenant Colonel "Red George" Macdonell
Lieutenant Colonel John Macdonell, Brock's aide de camp
Sir George Prevost, the governor general of Canada
Lieutenant Colonel Henry Proctor
Major General Phineas Riall
General Roger Sheafe
Major General John Vincent

Canadians
Charles-Michel D'Irumberry de Salaberry
Captain Francois Ducharme
Matthew Elliott
Billy Green, the Scout
David and Jacob Manning
Captain William Hamilton Merritt
Colonel Murray
Lieutenant Frederic Roulette
Laura Secord

Native Peoples
Robert Dixon
John Norton
The Prophet
Tecumseh
Chief Walk in Water

Prologue

November 20, 1813

Dear Cousin Mary,
I wish you were here. It seems like forever since you last visited.
I know it was a little less than a year ago, but it seems like lon-
ger. It has become unbearable here. Papa is so strict. He refuses
to let me leave the farm anymore. He says it's too dangerous.
The American soldiers are everywhere. Papa says they are
our enemy.

Imagine! You're an American. Am I to think of you as
an enemy now? I'm sure it seems very silly to you, but terrible
things have been happening. Do you remember the Morriseys?
Their farm was burned to the ground last week. A group of
American soldiers set it on fire. The same thing happened to
the Wiersdmas. Then the Smith boys refused to join the militia,
and they were arrested.

I long for last summer. We had so much fun together.
This silly war seemed like such an adventure then. Now I'm
frightened. Mother cries a lot. She's worried about my brothers.
They're with the militia down near Queenston.

I really hope the war is over soon. I'm sure this all seems
very far away to you in New Orleans. I trust it stays far away
from you.

Keep us in your thoughts.

Your cousin,
Sarah

Twelve Mile Creek, Upper Canada

Chapter 1
1812: Isaac Brock

Major General Isaac Brock was a soldier without a war to fight. He had lived in Canada for 10 long years waiting for a war. Nothing had happened. All he wanted was to be allowed to go home to Britain. He wanted to be where the real action was. Other British soldiers were fighting against Napoleon. He wanted to fight alongside them. Every time he asked to go home, his superiors said no.

Brock was blonde, blue-eyed, and well over six feet tall. He looked very handsome in his scarlet uniform. At 42, he was the commander-in-chief of all the British troops in Upper Canada. He had proved himself in battle. His men respected and admired him. He was seen as a man with a destiny. Could he find his destiny in Canada? Brock didn't think so.

In the early 19th century, Canada was called **The Canadas**. There were two provinces called Upper Canada and Lower Canada (modern-day Ontario and Quebec). The people who lived there were called colonials. They lived mostly in small villages along the border with the United States. Most colonials were farmers. Many were recent immigrants from the United States. They were called Loyalists. They had fled to Canada after the American War of Independence (1775–1783).

The border between the United States and Canada was open. People of both countries crossed back and forth whenever they wanted. There were forts along the border, but most were falling apart. Nothing much happened in these forts. Few soldiers remained at each one. They spent their time talking about past battles and waiting for something exciting to happen.

In 1812, Brock received permission to return to England. He should have been thrilled. However, things were becoming more exciting in Canada.

Whispers of War
The colonials had whispered of war with the Americans for a long time. Now, it looked like the rumours might be true. Some members of the American government were openly calling for war. Many believed that a war with Canada would hardly be a war at all. Thomas Jefferson, a former American president, declared that invading Canada would be "a mere matter of marching."

So it might have been. There were seven million Americans at that time. They had 35,000 men in their army and plenty of weapons. There were barely half a million Canadians. Defending The Canadas were 5,000 British soldiers and 4,000 volunteer soldiers called **militia**. They had very few weapons.

Brock worried about the Canadian militia. Few of these volunteers had any deep attachment to Britain. Fewer still could be counted on to commit to a war they saw as a fight between the British and Americans. He believed the militia lacked training. He thought they would desert at the first opportunity. Brock would soon change his mind about Canadian fighting men.

War!
On June 19, 1812, Brock was having dinner with some American generals at Fort George. Suddenly, one of his aides burst in with news for him. America had declared war on Canada. Brock and the generals politely finished their meals. Then they returned to their headquarters to plot strategy. Word spread quickly. No one doubted the outcome. Canadian politicians, colonials, and Native peoples all believed the Americans would win.

It seemed that no one had counted on Isaac Brock. "Most of the people have lost confidence," he wrote to one of his brothers. "I, however, speak loud and look big."

Brock the Bold

Isaac Brock was a natural leader. He was known for his boldness and quick thinking. His ability to bluff was legendary. In his youth, he had been challenged to a duel. He said that he would fight the duel, but not at the usual 30 paces. Instead, he and his opponent would fire at each other, face to face, over a handkerchief. His opponent quickly backed down.

Brock's quick thinking helped even the odds with the Americans before the first shot had even been fired. Brock sent out couriers right away. They were to tell his fort commanders that the war had started. One courier went to Fort Amherstberg. (It is now called Fort Malden, present-day Amherstberg, Ontario.) Just as he was giving the news to the soldiers there, an American schooner called the *Cuyahoga Packet* sailed by. Frederic Roulette was a young French-Canadian lieutenant at the fort. Roulette ordered a British captain and six sailors into a longboat. The men approached the *Cuyahoga Packet*. They boarded her and told the captain and crew they were prisoners of war. The Americans were stunned. They did not know that war had even been declared.

The *Cuyahoga Packet* had been carrying letters from William Hull. He was an American general. While the Americans were being taken prisoner, Hull was hiking through the forests of western Michigan. He was on his way to Fort Detroit. He had no idea that the war had started either.

Brock read the letters from Hull. His letters confirmed what Brock had already suspected. Once Hull reached Fort Detroit, he would launch an attack. It would be directed at the village of Sandwich, near Fort Amherstberg. The letters also revealed other important information for Brock. Hull had a very small army. He thought the Canadians had more weapons. He didn't want to fight a war against Canada. He also wrote that he was terrified of fighting the Native peoples.

Brock knew it would take Hull at least four weeks to reach Fort Detroit. Brock planned to pay him a visit there. In the meantime, he had another battle to put in motion.

Robert Dixon was born in Scotland. He had married a Sioux woman and thought of himself as a Sioux warrior. On July 17, Dixon got his orders from Brock. Dixon, 250 warriors, and a few retired soldiers and fur traders waited until it was dark. Then they silently paddled across Lake Huron to Michilimackinac Island. They quietly woke up the villagers and took them to safety. Then Dixon confronted Porter Hanks, the American commander at Fort Michilimackinac. Hanks was terrified at the sight of the native warriors. He surrendered the fort.

The British, the Canadians, and their native allies had won the first battle. Not a single shot had been fired! Brock shared the wealth from the captured fort with his native friends. This was a wise move. It sent a clear message to the Native peoples. The British were willing to fight. They were able to win, and they offered rewards.

Brock wanted to be with Dixon or fighting General Hull in Detroit. Instead, he was in York (present-day Toronto, Ontario). He needed more men and more arms. He had to convince the government in York to give them to him.

Hull had already occupied the town of Sandwich. Brock expected him to attack Fort Amherstberg at any moment. Brock's superior, Sir George Prevost, was the governor general of Canada. Sir Prevost was trying to negotiate peace. The war might be over before Brock had a chance to see any action!

In early August, the government agreed to allow Brock to call up the militia. Finally, Brock was given the men he needed. Five hundred Canadians answered his call. But there weren't enough weapons or supplies. Brock could only take half the men with him.

Brock and his army travelled by sailboat across Lake Erie. On their way, they were caught in a storm. When the storm died, so did the wind. The men had to row the rest of the way. Brock's boat hit a rock. In full dress, he climbed overboard to help move it. At last, the group was able to continue. Brock opened his personal stock of spirits. He handed a glass to every man on board. This generous act was one of many. Brock became a hero to his men.

Once they had landed, Brock told the tired soldiers to sleep. He and a few men kept going to Fort Amherstberg. It was long past midnight when he reached the fort. Before he had a chance to fall into bed, there was a loud knock at his door. Outside was Lieutenant Colonel John Macdonell. He was Brock's aide de camp. Standing next to Macdonell was a tall, thin warrior named Tecumseh.

Brock and Tecumseh eyed each other. Tecumseh saw a tall, broad-shouldered soldier. He also saw a man of intelligence and action, a leader like himself. "Here is a man!" he later exclaimed to his fellow chiefs.

Brock was also impressed. The two men shook hands. Brock called a hasty war conference. Brock's superiors had ordered him to act only if he was attacked. Brock's junior officers wanted him to be careful. Tecumseh pushed for immediate action. Brock agreed with Tecumseh.

Brock the Brash

On August 15, Brock ordered his soldiers to fire on Fort Detroit. Then he demanded that the Americans surrender. Hull was safe within the walls of the fort with his soldiers. He refused to surrender.

Brock had 500 native warriors, 700 Canadians, and barely 300 British soldiers. He knew his men were hopelessly outnumbered. However, Brock had a plan. Brock sent Tecumseh and 500 of his **Shawnee** warriors to the fort. They stayed hidden in the forest around the fort and waited.

Brock ordered the British soldiers to give the militia their spare uniforms. There were not enough uniforms to go around. They shared them — a bright red jacket here, a pair of white breeches there. Brock organized the men into columns and ordered them to march at twice the usual distance from one another. To the Americans watching from the fort, Brock's ragtag army looked twice as big as it really was.

Brock rode at the head of the line. His great height and red and gold uniform made him an easy target. An aide suggested that Brock would be safer somewhere within the column. Brock refused. He would not ask his men to go where he was not willing to lead.

The British came within range of the American guns. Then Brock turned and led his men into the safety of a nearby ravine. Brock remembered that General Hull was afraid of native warriors. He ordered Tecumseh to parade his troops across a field in full view of the fort. The warriors crossed the field and disappeared into the forest. Then they came back. Over and over again, they marched. General Hull thought he was facing 1,500 warriors.

Hull was terrified. He asked for a three-day **truce**. Brock gave him three hours. Then Brock said that he doubted he could control the warriors once the fighting began. Hull had heard and seen enough. He surrendered.

Brock and Tecumseh rode into the fort side by

side. Both men looked impressive. Brock wore a beaded sash tied around his waist. The sash was a gift from Tecumseh. Tecumseh wore his fringed buckskin. It is said that Brock had given Tecumseh his own military sash. Tecumseh had given it to another chief he considered to be more important.

Brock had won again. Most of the Michigan Territory was in British hands. Many of the Native peoples were ready to join the British. The militia and the Upper Canada **legislature** were also excited by Brock's success.

Canadians began to think there was a chance they could win this war. Brock had captured an entire army. It was an army that was twice as big as his own. With the capture of Fort Detroit, the British and Canadians had control of the Michigan Territory. This territory was as large as Upper Canada. The capture of Detroit brought Brock's army weapons, supplies, and money. These thrilled him more than having control of the territory.

Brock knew that the war had just begun. He also knew that the American's best chance of success was to attack in several places. He figured the next attack would take place on the Niagara frontier (near present-day Niagara Falls). He hurried to meet them.

Before Brock reached Niagara, he heard news that threatened everything. Governor General George Prevost had arranged a one-month truce with the Americans. The truce had gone into effect on August 8, a week before Brock had taken Fort Detroit. No word had reached the British or the Americans there. Brock was bitterly disappointed. The Native peoples were angry. Had they backed the wrong side?

In Niagara, Brock was hailed as a hero. He used his new hero status to convince the government to give him more men. He could not convince his superiors to let him attack the Americans again.

In America, Brock was also called a hero. They had heard about his victories. They had also heard about his honour. Earlier in the war, a Canadian commander had raided several American farms. Brock was furious. He sent the commander back to the farms. Brock ordered the commander to return everything he had taken.

A Thin Red Line

Brock believed the Americans were using the truce to prepare an attack. He spread his tiny army along the 37-mile Niagara border. He sent most of them to Fort Erie and Chippewa. Everyone expected the Americans to attack there first.

Brock arrived in Fort George (Niagara-on-the-Lake, Ontario) on September 6. It was two days before the truce was supposed to end. Waiting for him along the border were 8,000 American soldiers.

Brock asked for more soldiers. Governor General Prevost refused. He didn't want to upset the peace. He didn't believe there would be a war. He suggested that Brock leave the Michigan Territory and use those soldiers. Brock knew he couldn't. His victory in Detroit had brought him the support of the Canadian people and the Native peoples. Leaving that territory could lose him that support.

Brock was first and foremost a soldier. He obeyed commands. He believed he could win, but he did not attack. Nor did he abandon the Michigan Territories.

Brock was frustrated. He knew the Americans would have to attack soon to keep their troops under control. A number of American soldiers had already defected to the British. The American militia was no happier with the war than the Canadians were. Most didn't want to fight their former neighbours. Militia pay and rations offered them little reason to fight.

Brock set up a system of beacon signals along the Niagara frontier. He would use these signals to warn of the coming attack. Then he waited.

A few soldiers were stationed at the village of Queenston. It was located 10 kilometres south of Fort George. On the night of October 11, they listened to the Americans try and fail to invade Queenston. The Americans were armed and anxious to start the fight. They had boarded boats to take them across the Niagara River to the village. To their dismay, they discovered that all the oars had been stored onboard another boat. That boat had disappeared, along with the sailor in charge of it. They were stranded.

The Americans and Canadians sat out the night

behind their own borders. Outside, a huge storm whipped up the rough waters of the river. The wait took its toll on the soldiers of both sides. In the morning, Brock received word from his soldiers in Queenston. They threatened to shoot their superiors if action did not begin soon. Brock sent a trusted officer to investigate the **mutiny**. That officer was Captain Thomas Evans.

Evans reported that he had released all the mutinying soldiers in Queenston. He believed the group could earn their parole in the coming fight. The officer also told Brock that he believed the Americans were getting ready to attack Queenston.

Brock's staff officers dismissed Evans' report. They had been hearing rumours of an attack for a month. Brock wasn't so sure. He told his soldiers in Queenston to be ready. The Grenadiers were in a stone guardhouse in the village. The Light Company was camped atop the hill above the village. With the militia and regulars, a mere 300 men guarded Queenston.

Brock the Brave

At 4 a.m. the next morning, the booming of American cannons awakened Brock in his quarters in Fort George. They were firing on Queenston. Had the battle begun? Was Queenston the true target? Or, was this a trick to draw attention away from the real attack on Fort George?

Brock decided to see for himself. He ordered a small group of soldiers and **Mohawk** warriors to follow him. Then he jumped on his horse and rode toward Queenston. His aide de camp, Macdonell, raced after his general. He could not catch him. Two other aides had not even had time to dress. They were even farther behind.

Brock struggled through the mud on the ride to Queenston. On the way, he ran into a young York militiaman. He had been sent to tell Brock the enemy had launched their attack. In the heat of battle, no one had thought of using Brock's carefully planned signal fires. Brock was angry that no one had used them. However, he was excited about the prospect of battle. He urged his horse forward. The York Volunteers were moving towards the village. Brock waved the militia unit on as he galloped past.

Queenston was a tidy little village with no more than 20 houses. As Brock rode into the village, the Grenadiers cheered him. He saw they were holding the enemy. He galloped past and headed directly for the hill above the village. There, the men of the Light Company were protecting the heights. As soon as he reached the top, Brock ordered these men to go back down the hill to help the Grenadiers.

Brock was left with an eight-man gunner team. The men aimed the 18-pound cannon at the American shore. Brock watched the scene below him. Cannons on both sides roared constantly. Shells burst in the air above the river and the village. The bright flare of muskets lit up the murky dawn. Across the water, he saw hundreds of the enemy. They were waiting their turn to board the boats and cross to Queenston. Shells splashed into the water around the sailors as they rowed empty boats back to the American side to pick up more men.

Then Brock heard a spine-chilling sound from behind him. It was a battle cry. He spun around to see an American force. Brock and the gunners destroyed their gun so the Americans could not use it. Then the gunners ran down the hill toward the Grenadiers. Brock quickly followed, leading his horse by the reins. He hadn't even had time to get back on his horse.

Brock hid in one of the abandoned houses in the village. By this time, Brock's aide de camp had reached the village. Macdonell found his general. Brock told him to send for **reinforcements**. The situation was desperate. He could try to retake the hill, but he didn't have enough men. The reinforcements would not arrive until it was too late. The Americans would use that time to ferry over more men. Without control of the hill, Brock believed Upper Canada would be lost. Once the Americans gained a foothold in Queenston, they would have cut the Niagara frontier and Brock's army in two.

Brock didn't hesitate long. He mounted his horse and galloped through the village. He rallied some 200 soldiers and an equal number of weary local militia. The militia were men he was now proud to lead.

"Follow me boys," he yelled, as he thundered toward the base of the hill. A moment later, he shouted,

"Take a breath. You'll need it in a few moments."

The soldiers cheered. Before the cheers had died away, Brock charged up the hill. His soldiers struggled to keep up on the slippery footing of wet leaves. No one was close enough to their general to urge him to slow down and take cover among them. Once again, Brock was an easy target. This time, he took a bullet in his wrist. The wound slowed him down, but he pressed on, waving his sword.

On the hill above them, the Americans had spread out. They hid among the trees. They kept firing at the British and Canadian soldiers as they came up the hill. Many bullets found their mark. One found Brock.

"Are you much hurt, sir?" one of the militiamen asked.

Brock did not reply. His hand clutched his chest as he sank to the ground. The bullet had pierced his heart. He died instantly.

The stunned soldiers crowded around their fallen leader. They couldn't believe their hero was dead. They retreated, carrying Brock's body back down the hill.

Even in death, Brock was a leader. The British and Canadian soldiers wanted revenge. They wanted control of the hill for Brock. Macdonell led two more attempts to retake the hill. Both were unsuccessful. He was wounded in the second attack and died later that night.

More soldiers finally arrived. They joined Brock's troops in the fight. Together, they pushed the Americans out of the village. On the hill, General Roger Sheafe led the British toward the American line. The Americans fled to the edge of the hill. Some fell to their deaths. Others managed to make it to the beach. There, they waited for boats that never came. Many others hid in caves and waited for their leader to surrender.

He tried. The American commander sent two men on separate missions to surrender. Both were killed by angry native warriors. They had seen the Americans kill their men. Finally, the commander went himself. He made it through, barely. His surrender was accepted.

Brock's forces had won the day. They recaptured the heights and the village. Three hundred Americans were killed or wounded, and 925 were taken prisoner. The British and Canadians suffered only 15 deaths and 70 wounded. However, the victory was a sad one. Their hero, Brock, was dead.

On the morning of October 16, the caskets of Brock and Macdonell were carried from Government House in Newark to Fort George. Hundreds of people came out to watch the solemn procession. Inside the fort, more than 5,000 troops, militia, and native warriors stood in rows. The soldiers paid their final respects as the pallbearers carried the two caskets between the rows.

Brock and Macdonell were lowered into a single grave. A 21-gun salute broke the silence. Moments later, soldiers on the American side echoed the salute. They shot their guns to pay their respects to the fallen general.

Far away in England, church bells rang in Sir Isaac Brock's memory. He had been made a Knight of the Order of Bath for his capture of Fort Detroit. Brock never learned of the honour.

Brock's home town was on the small island of Guernsey, Channel Islands. There, his family crest was changed to include the figure of a native warrior. This change honoured Brock's friendship with Tecumseh and the Native peoples of Canada.

In one short year, Brock had managed to inspire a nation. He was a legend. After his death, the legend of Brock became larger than the man himself. He had wanted nothing more than to leave Canada. Instead, Brock's destiny was to spend all of eternity there as a symbol of loyalty and courage.

For Tecumseh and the native warriors, Brock's death was a terrible blow. They had lost the one British soldier they admired and trusted. He was the man who had promised them a homeland. Still, they had made their decision. They would remain with the British to see the war to its end.

Few others had shared Brock's confidence that Canada could repel the Americans. With his death, Canadians had a hero to mourn. They also had a common cause to rally behind. They had learned to have confidence in their leaders and themselves.

They were going to need both in the coming months.

Chapter 2
1813–1814:
James Fitzgibbon

Until the fall of 1812, the war didn't bother most Canadians and Americans. Farmers in Upper and Lower Canada kept selling their goods in American markets. American farmers supplied much of the beef eaten by British soldiers. The battles were fought by soldiers around forts. Very few people had died. Villagers had been left in peace. That all changed after October 13, 1812.

Many Canadian militiamen had died alongside Brock at the Battle of Queenston Heights. In the months that followed, the Canadians and British would win one battle. Then they would lose the next. No one was really sure who controlled what territory. Soldiers sometimes became separated from their units. They roamed the frontier, not knowing which side of the border they were on.

The people of Upper Canada were now living in a battleground. Their farms were burned. Their possessions were taken. Their men were forced to join the Canadian militia or imprisoned by the Americans. Soon all Canadians were forced to choose sides. Some sided with the Americans. Most stood firm as Canadians.

The bravery of some of these men helped turn the tide of the war in Canada's favour. Lieutenant James Fitzgibbon was fortunate. He crossed paths with two of these brave Canadians: Billy "The Scout" Green and Laura Secord.

James Fitzgibbon, the Soldier
Lieutenant James Fitzgibbon was a self-educated man. He had been promoted because of his skills. He was a favourite of General Brock. Like Brock, he was a natural leader. He earned the respect and loyalty of his men with ease. Fitzgibbon wanted to form a special unit of soldiers. He went to ask his commanding officer, Major General John Vincent. Because of the respect the men had for Fitzgibbon, Major General Vincent allowed him to form this special unit. Fitzgibbon hand-picked the men. He trained them in guerrilla warfare. Their task was to chase down the American soldiers who were burning and looting Canadian farms.

The unit called themselves "The Bloody Boys." Canadians loved The Bloody Boys. They roamed the Niagara region on horseback. Often, they travelled in disguise. Stories of their adventures encouraged some people to help them.

In April 1813, American warships sailed across Lake Ontario. The soldiers invaded and destroyed Fort York. Then they went on to loot the town of York (present-day Toronto, Ontario.) A month later, they turned their attention to the south. They began another attack on Fort George, where Fitzgibbon was.

The young lieutenant was forced to abandon the fort, along with 1,400 other men and their commander, John Vincent. They marched inland towards Beaver Dams. There, they were joined by other British troops. Some of these troops were escaping from Fort Erie at the southern end of the Niagara frontier. The other troops were escaping from Amherstberg on the western frontier. Retreat was the only possible choice, so Vincent sent the Canadian militia back to their homes. It made little sense to keep housing and feeding a volunteer army during a retreat. Many of them were needed at home on their farms.

The Americans chased the retreating British for four weeks. The Canadians believed that the British were abandoning them. In fact, Vincent had been ordered to abandon this part of the Canadas. His superiors did not think it was important. Nor did they think he could defend it. However, the people of Niagara were fortunate. Vincent was not willing to give up the area without a fight.

Once the troops were off the peninsula, Vincent halted his retreat. He set up camp at Burlington Heights (near present-day Hamilton, Ontario.) The British had barely 1,600 men. They were about to face nearly 3,000 Americans. They needed an edge. The daring James Fitzgibbon was just the man to give them that edge.

On the morning of June 5, Fitzgibbon dressed himself as a butter peddler. He entered the American camp. While he sold his butter, he counted both the men and their weapons. Then he returned to his own camp. He reported that the Americans were not organized. Their men and guns were badly positioned. He had also found out the Americans were expecting more soldiers to arrive soon. He advised Vincent to attack right away.

Billy Green, the Scout

At the same time, two young farmers — Billy Green and his brother Levi — were roaming the woods on the Niagara Escarpment. They were out on a morning walk. The last thing they expected to see was the American army.

The Green family had moved to Canada from the United States 19 years earlier. They had moved just before Billy's birth. Until that day, Billy had only one claim to fame. He was the first white child born in Stoney Creek. He would soon have another claim to fame.

The brothers were not interested in the position

or strength of the army. They wanted to have a little fun with the Americans. They hid in the trees and watched as the American advance guard marched by. The boys began whooping like warriors. The Americans were terrified. The boys laughed as the stragglers at the end of the American column ran to catch up to the rest of the troop.

"I tell you, those simple fellows did run," Billy said years later.

When the coast was clear, Billy and Levi made their way to the village. They crossed the road the American troops had just marched along. They came across a lone American soldier. He was winding a rag around his bootless foot. The American reached for his gun, but Levi was quicker. He grabbed a stick and struck the soldier. The other soldiers heard their comrade's yells and began firing. Billy and Levi disappeared into the woods and ran back up the ridge.

The brothers reached Levi's cabin safely. By then, other settlers had heard the sound of war whoops and gunfire. A crowd had come out onto the hill to see what was happening. Billy and Levi joined them. They watched as the Americans walked through the village. Billy could not resist a repeat performance. He whooped again, and Levi answered him. One of the Americans fired at the hill. The shot almost hit Levi's wife and baby.

Billy and Levi hid in the woods. Levi's wife hid in a

nearby trapper's hut. A group of soldiers knocked at the trapper's door. They asked if she had seen any native warriors. In a trembling voice, she told them a fierce band of warriors was roaming the mountain. The soldiers were convinced and left quickly.

Once the Americans had gone, Billy went to Stoney Creek. He wanted to check on his sister, Keziah Corman, and her husband, Isaac. Keziah told him that Isaac had been arrested. He had answered rudely when the Americans asked for directions. Billy ran through the village and into the woods in search of his brother-in-law. As he ran, he whistled like a bird. It was a signal. At last, his whistles were answered by an owl hoot. It was Isaac.

Isaac had made his escape by pretending he was an American. He had convinced them that he supported their cause. The commander had released Isaac right away. He had even given Isaac the password so the soldiers would allow him through their lines.

Isaac had sworn not to give the password to the British — so he did not. He gave it to Billy instead. Billy wanted to do his part for Canada. He borrowed a horse and started out for Burlington Heights. He was going to give the password to the British. He rode the horse until it was exhausted. Then he walked the rest of the way.

Billy arrived late that night. Vincent was ready to attack the Americans, but he was worried. There were far more American soldiers. More were expected at any time. They had also had word that the Americans were expecting their warships to arrive soon. It seemed the British had only one chance. They would surprise the Americans under cover of darkness.

At first, the British suspected Billy of being a spy. Soon they believed his story. They took him to Vincent's commanding officer, Lieutenant Colonel John Harvey. Billy gave him the password. He also told Harvey where and how the Americans were camped. Harvey asked Billy if he could lead them.

Billy galloped off towards Stoney Creek with the British behind him. From time to time, he grew frustrated with the soldiers lagging behind him. He went back to urge them to move more quickly.

"It will be daylight soon," he urged.

"That will be soon enough to be killed," one of the men replied.

They reached the American camp just before dawn. Billy killed one sentry with his knife. Another guard managed to fire a shot. It alerted his fellow soldiers. The British dashed forward, whooping like native warriors as they fired their muskets. The Americans met them. The line of battle blurred in the darkness. It was hard to tell enemy from friend. The British line faltered until Fitzgibbon appeared to restore order. Finally, two American generals were captured. The cannons were disabled. The American troops scattered in retreat.

Cyrenius Chapin, the Raider

For three days, Vincent's troops followed the Americans to Fort George. Luckily, they often came across wagon-loads of supplies. They had been left behind by the fleeing Americans. At last, the British and Canadians stood before the wooden palisades of the fort. They could not get in. The fort was too heavily defended.

From time to time, the Americans managed to escape the fort to make raids on nearby farms and villages. Cyrenius Chapin was one of the men in these raiding parties. He was a doctor from Buffalo, New York. The doctor was well known for his ruthless plundering of the homes of local settlers. Fitzgibbon was disgusted by Chapin's rampages. He was determined to put an end to them. He knew Chapin was in the fort. Fitzgibbon was just waiting for a chance to capture him.

That chance came on June 19. Fitzgibbon heard that the doctor had slipped out of the fort with a raiding party. Fitzgibbon and his Bloody Boys began searching the Niagara Peninsula for him. They tracked the raiding party to the countryside around the village of Lundy's Lane (present-day Niagara Falls, Ontario). It was almost halfway down the peninsula. Fitzgibbon believed he would attract less attention on his own. He told his men to wait outside the village.

Fitzgibbon started into the village. The wife of a local militiaman waved him down. She told him that Chapin was just ahead with more than 200 men. She urged Fitzgibbon to flee to safety. Fitzgibbon was not prepared to retreat. His enemy was near. He was not about to let him go.

Fitzgibbon spotted a horse that belonged to one of the raiders. It was tied to a post outside a tavern. He went into the tavern. Two raiders attacked him. One aimed a rifle at him. Fitzgibbon pretended to know the raider. He extended a hand toward the man as if he planned to shake his hand. This action confused the American just long enough. Fitzgibbon seized his rifle and ordered him to surrender. The other American took aim, but Fitzgibbon grabbed his rifle before he could fire.

A struggle followed. The three men tumbled out of the tavern. The woman who had warned Fitzgibbon about the raiders was still on the road. She pleaded for help from several passing wagons. The drivers did not want to get involved. Only a small boy answered her plea. He threw stones at the Americans. One of the raiders grabbed hold of Fitzgibbon's sword. Would this be the end of Fitzgibbon? The innkeeper's wife had rushed outside to watch the fight, still holding her baby. When she saw that Fitzgibbon was in danger, she put the baby down. She ran forward and kicked the sword from the American's hand. Then she scooped up her baby and disappeared into the tavern. Finally, the innkeeper arrived. He helped Fitzgibbon disarm and arrest the Americans.

But Dr. Chapin escaped.

Laura Secord, the Heroine of Beaver Dams

A few days later, Vincent ordered Fitzgibbon to a house near Beaver Dams. It was on the ridge, about 30 kilometres southwest of Fort George. Fitzgibbon and the Bloody Boys were still looking for Dr. Chapin and other raiders. They would use the house as their headquarters.

Meanwhile, the Americans were still trapped inside Fort George. They grew more and more frustrated at not being able to break free. They were also frustrated with Fitzgibbon and his Bloody Boys. They had been a nuisance for long enough. American spies soon found out where Fitzgibbon was. The commander at the fort sent out a message for more troops to come to their aid. The plan was that the troops would attack the hated Fitzgibbon first. Then they would rescue the Americans at the fort. The rescuing troops were soon on their way. They were led by Lieutenant Colonel Charles Boerstler.

A small **advance party** of Boerstler's men stopped in Queenston to wait for the rest of the force. They chose a house at random. They demanded that the homeowners, James and Laura Secord, serve them dinner.

Laura Secord and her husband James were both children of **United Empire Loyalists**. Their families had fled to Canada during the American War of Independence almost 40 years before. James owned a shop, and the family was fairly wealthy.

James had fought in the battle of Queenston

Heights. When he hadn't returned, Laura had gone to the battlefield to find him. He had been shot in the kneecap and shoulder. He was in grave condition. Laura had begged the help of a passing soldier. Together, they had brought James home. James had lived, but his war service was over.

No more battles were being fought in Queenston. However, American soldiers often looted the homes. Sometimes, they burned them to the ground. By the time Boerstler's men burst into the Secord home, it had already been raided twice.

The first time, Laura had protected the family heirloom, a rare collection of Spanish coins. She had tossed them into a boiling pot of water hanging over the kitchen fire. The second time, one of the American soldiers had boasted about returning to claim the Secord property after they had chased away the British. Laura was furious. She told him there was only one piece of land in Queenstown he would ever be able to claim. That would be a six-foot grave. His companions returned later that day. They told Laura that her words had come true. The man had been killed in a skirmish with Canadian soldiers.

Laura was furious that the soldiers had returned but she gave in to their demand for dinner. She had no choice. Her husband was still in bed recovering from his wounds. There was no Canadian militia nearby. The evening wore on, and the Americans grew bolder. They bragged that they were planning a surprise attack on Fitzgibbon. They also talked about their grand plans to open up the entire peninsula to a massive American attack.

Laura had no details of how or when the attack would take place. However, she knew that Fitzgibbon was Canada's best chance for holding Niagara. She also knew that he had to be warned. Her husband was too badly injured to go. She would have to make the long journey.

The next day dawned very hot. Laura rose early. She put on a long cotton dress and white bonnet. Light slippers with low heels covered her feet. They would not offer much protection on her journey, but they also would not raise any suspicion among the Americans. Laura did not want to be caught. The penalty for spying was death by firing squad. As dawn broke, she set out for her sister-in-law's home in the nearby village of St. David's. She carried a small basket of preserves.

Along the way, Laura was stopped twice by American patrols. She told them that she was going to visit her sick brother in St. David's. This part of her story was true. Charles Ingersoll was recovering from a fever. The soldiers knew this, so they let her pass.

If her brother was too ill to go to Fitzgibbon, Laura was hoping that one of her older nephews would go instead. When she got to St. David's later that morning, she found that Charles was still feverish. Worse still, the boys had both joined the Canadian militia. She would have to make the 25-kilometre journey herself.

Laura walked on the road as far as the village of Shipman's Corners (present-day St. Catherines, Ontario). Then she travelled cross-country to avoid American patrols. She waded through the Black Swamp. This area was home to rattlesnakes, wolves, and wildcats. It took all afternoon to cross the swamp. She suffered terribly from the heat. Her courage almost failed her when she heard first one, then several wolf howls. It was early evening when she reached the edge of the swamp. She was ragged, shoeless, and exhausted. She still had a long way to go.

Laura was climbing a steep hill. She realized she was being watched. She didn't stop. She pushed on through the thick brush. At the edge of a clearing, she found herself surrounded by a group of **Caughnawaga** warriors. Luckily, the warriors were loyal to the British. Their chief sent two warriors to escort Laura to Fitzgibbon. They arrived at Fitzgibbon's house just before midnight. Laura had been walking for almost 18 hours.

Fitzgibbon acted on Laura's information right away. He sent the Caughnawaga warriors to watch for the American advance. The lieutenant was grateful. He marvelled at Laura's courage. Years later, he would still talk of the debt he owed her. People who supported the Americans lived in Laura's village. Therefore, no one could know of Laura's brave deed. She could be killed because of what she had done.

After the war, Laura broke her silence about her brave walk. She did so in order to get some compensation from the British. James had lost his shop. He could not find work because of his war injuries. Laura sent many letters. Fitzgibbon wrote a glowing letter of support. Local politicians finally offered James Secord the position of magistrate. In 1860, the Prince of Wales granted Laura a reward of £100 (about $200). She was 83 years old.

The Battle of Beaver Dams

Finally, Boerstler and the rest of his men reached Queenston. He put patrols in place to make sure that no one escaped to warn the British. He didn't know it was already too late. The next morning, the Americans marched to St. David's.

The Caughnawaga **scouts** warned their French Canadian commander, Francoise Ducharme. He sent them on to warn Fitzgibbon.

The Americans stopped on the Niagara ridge. It lay along a narrow strip of land lined on both sides by dense forest. The area was known as Beaver Dams.

Ducharme led several hundred warriors in an attack on the Americans. Ducharme's Caughnawagas were supported by several dozen Mohawks. They fired from the forest. Boerstler's troops returned fire. The heavy fire from the forests showed no sign of letting up. The tired soldiers knew they were vulnerable.

Meanwhile, Fitzgibbon had been hidden in the forest. He was waiting for his reinforcements to arrive before he joined the fight. Fitzgibbon had only 44 Bloody Boys with him. The reinforcements were nowhere in sight. The Americans couldn't know that. Fitzgibbon decided to bluff. He walked out carrying a white flag and demanded that Boerstler surrender. He told the American that the British had his troops completely surrounded. He also added the lie that had been told and retold. The native warriors would massacre the Americans unless they surrendered at once. Boerstler refused. He wasn't going to surrender to an army he had not even seen.

Fitzgibbon then made a suggestion. The Americans could send an officer to inspect the strength of the British troops. He went back into the forest. He pretended that he was going to ask his superior to allow an American officer to see the troops. At this point, Fitzgibbon got lucky. His plan was to get a British officer in full uniform to pose as his superior. However, he did not have a single British officer in his party.

While he was trying to come up with another plan, the advance party of his reinforcements came crashing through the forest. Fitzgibbon was relieved. He ordered one of the British soldiers to play the part of commander. He did a brilliant job. He refused to allow the enemy to see his men. However, he assured Boerstler that there were more than enough of them to defeat the Americans.

Hearing this, Boerstler asked for time to decide. Fitzgibbon gave him five minutes. Again, he used the lie that he would not be able to control the native warriors for longer than that. Boerstler threw up his hands and begged to be saved from the warriors.

Fitzgibbon's bluff had worked.

Now Fitzgibbon faced another hurdle. He had to figure out how to disarm 500 Americans with only his band of Bloody Boys, a handful of warriors, and a dozen **dragoons**. Surrenders were usually very formal. The surrendering army had to hand their weapons to the captors. Of course, Fitzgibbon could not allow this. The Americans could not know how small their group really was. If they realized this, they would call off the surrender and continue the fight.

Fitzgibbon was thinking about his next move when his real commanding officer arrived. He led a small group of soldiers. He didn't listen to Fitzgibbon's concerns about showing the Americans how few men they had. He told Boerstler to march his troops between the British troops and lay their weapons on the ground. Fitzgibbon had to be quick-witted. He asked — in a very loud voice — if it was really a good idea to march the Americans past the angry warriors. The Americans tossed down their weapons at once.

The War Drags On

More than a year later, Fitzgibbon took part in the long,

bloody siege of Fort Erie. In three months, the British made three attempts to breech the walls of the fort. Each time, the American gunners drove them back. The British succeeded on the fourth attempt. However, they reached only one of the fort's inner bastions. Many of the British soldiers believed they would die. Even Fitzgibbon thought so. During the siege, he asked for a brief leave. He left the battle to marry his sweetheart. If he died, she would have his pension to comfort her.

The brave Fitzgibbon survived the battle of Fort Erie. Many other British soldiers were not as lucky. Three hundred and sixty-six British soldiers were killed or wounded. Five hundred and thirty-nine were taken prisoner or listed as missing. Against all odds, Fitzgibbon survived the entire war without serious injury. He returned to his wife. They made their home in the country he had fought for and loved. When his wife died in 1846, Fitzgibbon retired to England. There, he was made a knight of Windsor for his services to the Crown. For the rest of his life, he longed to return to Canada.

Chapter 3
1810–1813: Tecumseh

Brock fought to defend the British Empire. Fitzgibbon fought to protect the Canadian colony he had grown to love. Another of their allies was the great chief Tecumseh. He fought for the Native peoples.

The Shawnee Chief felt the loss of Brock deeply. Tecumseh and Brock were both brave and loyal. They shared a common goal. They wanted to defeat the Americans. Neither man had completely trusted the other. Brock used Tecumseh and the native warriors to win the war for the British. Tecumseh used the British for his own vision. He wanted to pursue a United Native Empire.

A Man of Many Parts
Tecumseh was born in the Ohio Territories around 1768.

His father had been killed in a battle with the settlers. Tecumseh was just six years old when his father died. His older brother, Cheesuaka, adopted him. He trained Tecumseh to be a warrior and a leader. He also told him not to trust the settlers.

During his youth, Tecumseh watched the American government take more and more land from his people. He became resentful. Then Cheesuaka died a violent death at the hands of the settlers. Tecumseh became dangerously bitter.

As an adult, Tecumseh warned his fellow peoples, "The white men aren't friends to the Indians ... At first they only asked for land sufficient for a wigwam; now, nothing will satisfy them but the whole of our hunting grounds from the rising to the setting sun."

Tecumseh took part in his first battle at the age of 15. He was a brave and ruthless warrior. He also had a more gentle side. He was still a young man when he watched a white prisoner being burned to death at the stake. He saved the man. He swore he would never again allow such horrible things in his presence.

When the war began, Tecumseh was 44 years old. He was a well-built man with handsome features. He looked frightening when he put on war paint. He could also appear as dignified as any British officer. His dignity showed when he delivered one of his famous speeches in English or Shawnee.

No picture exists of Tecumseh. He refused to have

his portrait painted. However, a wonderful description was written by one of Brock's aides. It paints a picture of its own. A ring, with "three small silver crowns, or coronets, were suspended from the lower cartilage of his aquiline nose; and a large silver medallion of George III ... was attached to a mixed coloured wampum string, and hung around his neck. His dress consisted of a plain, neat uniform, tanned deerskin jacket, with long trousers of the same material, the seams of both being covered with neatly cut fringe; and he had on his feet leather moccasins, much ornamented with work made from the dyed quills of the porcupine."

Not much is known about Tecumseh's personal life. He refused to drink alcohol. He was married four times. Finally, he chose to live without women in his life. Legend has it that as a young man, he fell in love with the 16-year-old daughter of a settler. It is said she taught him English. She also introduced him to the Bible and Shakespeare. His favourite play was *Hamlet.* The girl said she would marry him on one condition. He had to agree to give up his native ways. He refused.

War broke out between Canada and the United States in June 1812. By that time, Tecumseh was a man with only one passion: his cause.

A Dream of Nation

His cause was clear and noble. He dreamed of an "Indian Nation" stretching from the Great Lakes to the Gulf of

Mexico. He dreamed of uniting the Native peoples in a confederation. It would be similar to that of the United States. If anyone could achieve this, it was Tecumseh. He was a gifted speaker. He had convinced many of the native leaders to support his vision. Many supported his dream, but not all.

The British first met Tecumseh in 1810. They invited him to Fort Amherstberg. There, he was to meet Matthew Elliott, the Indian Department representative. Elliott had to find out if the Shawnee and other groups would be loyal to the British if war broke out with the Americans.

Elliott was a Loyalist. He had come to Canada after the American War of Independence. He had spent a lot of time with the Native peoples. He respected them. He had expected Tecumseh to be lukewarm about the idea of supporting the British. Elliott was surprised and pleased at Tecumseh's response. Tecumseh declared he was willing to fight the Americans. He had no interest in the quarrels between the settlers. However, he would strike at the Americans if they kept intruding on his land.

Tecumseh and his younger brother had been seeking support for their cause for several years. They had travelled among the different Native peoples in the United States and Upper and Lower Canada. They had encouraged them all to join the cause. Tecumseh and his brother were convincing men.

By 1811, more than 1,000 warriors had left their

homes to join the brothers. They gathered in a settlement where the Tippecanoe and Wabash rivers met. This settlement was near present-day Lafayette, Indiana.

Tecumseh's brother was known as the Prophet. He was the group's spiritual leader. He preached that the American settlers were a test from the Great Spirit. The Native peoples had to return to their old way of life. If not, they would risk losing everything. The settlers feared the Prophet. His own people admired him. The settlement was dubbed Prophet's Town.

The warriors and the Prophet needed military and political leadership. They looked to Tecumseh. He wanted to avoid bloodshed. He wanted to use words to stop the sale of land to the Americans. If his words failed, he was willing to use force. Tecumseh threatened to kill any chief who sold more land to the settlers.

Tippecanoe: A Catalyst to War

In the summer of 1811, several chiefs sold parts of their land to the Americans. The governor of Indian lands was William Harrison. He helped arrange the deal between the chiefs and the Americans. The governor knew that Tecumseh and his brother would be furious. He expected them to bother the settlers on the newly purchased land. He thought Tecumseh and his brother might even attack the settlers. Harrison invited the brothers to a meeting at his estate. It was near the town of Vincennes, Indiana.

Harrison planned the meeting carefully. He summoned the chiefs who had sold the land. He also called up a large group of soldiers to guard him. He hoped to scare off Tecumseh. He also hoped to impress Tecumseh with his importance. The governor arranged that he would be seated on stage. Tecumseh and his men would be seated below him. He had everything arranged by the planned date of the meeting. Then he waited and waited.

Tecumseh arrived on July 27 — three days late. He hadn't brought a small escort. Instead, 300 heavily armed warriors were with him. Harrison would soon learn that Tecumseh was not easily frightened or impressed. He refused to sit below Harrison. Instead, he sat on the ground some distance away. Harrison was forced to come to him.

Tecumseh argued that the chiefs had no right to sell the land. He said it belonged to all Native peoples. "Sell a country!" he exclaimed. "Why not sell the air, the clouds, and the great sea, as well as the earth? Did not Great Spirit make them all for the use of his children?"

Tecumseh was very angry. The assembly feared he would let his warriors attack Harrison. The warriors were held in check. They thundered away on their war ponies. Harrison was left nervous and impressed.

During the next two months, Harrison watched what was happening. More Native peoples flocked to Tecumseh and his brother at Prophet's Town. Tecumseh did not stay at the settlement. He kept travelling across the continent. The Native peoples were scattered across the land. Tecumseh wanted to find a way to unite them.

Finally, in the fall of 1811, Harrison made his move. Tecumseh was in the southern states. While he was gone, Harrison had a fort built in the Indiana territory. This was territory that Tecumseh and the Prophet said belonged to the Native peoples. It was a show of force. Harrison was also trying to lure the Prophet into battle while Tecumseh was gone. It didn't work.

In late October, Harrison began marching his army towards Prophet's Town. The Prophet thought the Americans were coming to destroy the settlement. On November 11, 1811, he attacked the Americans. Harrison's troops fought them off easily. This battle became known as the Battle of Tippecanoe. After their defeat, many of the native warriors began to think twice about supporting the Prophet and Tecumseh. Several hundred went back to their own lands. Others went into hiding, away from the settlement. Within two days of the Battle of Tippecanoe, Prophet's Town was completely deserted. Harrison's soldiers rode in. They burned it to the ground.

Tecumseh returned from his journey. He found Prophet's Town in ruins. He swore revenge on Harrison and all the Americans. The Americans didn't want Tecumseh as their enemy. They began to worry. They didn't want Tecumseh to join the British. They sent men to Tecumseh to try to win him over. He refused to listen.

Tecumseh decided to join the British. He sent runners to inform all the Native peoples. Twelve nations responded. Each sent two political chiefs and two war chiefs. By May of 1812, Tecumseh had recruited 600 men. They waited for the war to begin.

Joining the Battle

By the time war was declared, Tecumseh was already tracking the American armies. He reported their movements to the British. One of the armies Tecumseh tracked was lead by Brigadier General William Hull.

In July, Hull had crossed into Upper Canada from Fort Detroit. He had taken the village of Sandwich on Canada's western frontier. His next target was nearby Fort Amherstberg. He was not sure if he had enough men to take the fort. He had to find out. He sent out bands of militia to test the strength of the British. Tecumseh and his warriors were watching.

When the militia were halfway between Sandwich and Fort Amherstberg, Tecumseh's warriors swooped down on them. The soldiers were terrified. Against the orders of their officers, they retreated. The officers threatened to shoot the deserters. The soldiers said they would rather be shot by one of their own than killed by the warriors.

Tecumseh wasn't finished. On August 5, 1812, he

Brock and Tecumseh meet for the first time

crossed the border into Brownstown, Michigan. He attacked a wagon train carrying supplies for Hull's army. Hull heard about this attack and the capture of Fort Michilimackinac. He quickly fled Canada for the safety of Fort Detroit. Even there, he was not safe from Tecumseh.

Tecumseh captured a second supply train. Then he returned to Fort Amherstberg. There, he had his first meeting with General Brock. Within a few days, Tecumseh and his warriors helped capture Hull and Fort Detroit.

Hull lived out his days in disgrace. He blamed Tecumseh and his warriors for his defeat.

A Man of Principle

Tecumseh was a man of his word. He showed this at the surrender of Fort Detroit. He kept his promise to prevent a massacre. He was also caring. Stories of his kindness were told by soldiers on both sides of the border.

One story involved an American minister who had been captured at the surrender of Fort Detroit. Brock's deputy Lieutenant Colonel Henry Proctor had been put in charge of the surrender. The minister would not swear his loyalty to the British Crown. Proctor threatened to imprison the minister. Tecumseh felt this was wrong. He protested. Proctor ignored Tecumseh. The chief threatened to break his alliance with the British. Proctor gave in and released the minister.

Another story involved a young American boy. Tecumseh saw the boy tending two oxen. His men needed food, so he took the oxen. However, he promised to pay the family. Tecumseh asked the Indian Department representative to pay for the oxen. The department claimed the animals were spoils of war and refused to pay. Tecumseh insisted. He also demanded an extra dollar to pay for the boy's time and trouble in collecting payment. Tecumseh got his way.

The End of a Dream

It was the beginning of August, 1812. Tecumseh believed that his dream of a native confederacy would soon happen. He was allied with the winning side. He had finally convinced Walk-in-Water, a **Wyandot** chief, to cross to the British side. This was important to Tecumseh's vision. The Wyandot were a senior nation. Where they went, others would surely follow.

Then he heard that the British Governor General had arranged a ceasefire. Tecumseh was furious. His dream would never come true unless he could fight. He had to conquer the Americans. Like Brock, Tecumseh knew that the British and Native peoples had to strike then. If not, the Americans would use the time to their advantage. They would move more men and troops to the Niagara front or the western front.

Tecumseh was disgusted with his allies. He left the battlefront. The British didn't see him again that winter. However, Tecumseh realized his fortunes were tied to the British. He and his 2,000 men rejoined them at Amherstberg in the spring of 1813. There, he learned that Brock had been killed at Queenston Heights. Tecumseh was sorry to lose a man he respected. Brock's death worried him. What would it mean for his dream of a native confederacy? To add to his misery, he knew he had to be loyal to the man who would take Brock's place — Lieutenant Colonel Henry Proctor. Tecumseh did not like or respect Proctor.

Men of Lesser Valour
Tecumseh returned in the spring of 1813. Before that, Proctor had crossed the frozen Detroit River to launch

a counterattack against the Americans. The attack was to take place at the Canadian settlement of River Raisin (present-day Monroe, Michigan). With Proctor were native warriors led by Roundhead, a Wyandot chief. The battle was short and savage. The British took 500 American prisoners. However, Proctor was nervous. Almost right away, he retreated to the village of Brownstown. He felt safer there. He left the American prisoners in the hands of Roundhead and his warriors.

Tecumseh was not there to keep order. Roundhead's warriors murdered many of the prisoners. They held the others for ransom.

"Remember the River Raisin!" became a rallying cry for the American militia.

The Lull before the Storm
In the meantime, Governor Harrison had become a Brigadier General. In October 1812, he took command of the American Army of the Northwest. He ordered a fort to be built at Meigs, across the lake from Fort Amherstberg. It was one of the strongest forts of its time.

In early May 1813, Tecumseh and Proctor were sent to Fort Meigs. They had a combined force of 3,000 men. The big guns of the British did little damage to the fort's thick walls. Tecumseh and his men couldn't break into the fort.

A few days later, American reinforcements arrived by boat. Tecumseh sent a handful of warriors to get their attention. The massacre of River Raisin was still fresh in the Americans' minds. Half the reinforcements chased the warriors. They followed the warriors deep into the forest.

It was a trap. Tecumseh was waiting there with the rest of his men. By the time the fight was over, 650 Americans had been killed or captured. The warriors marched the prisoners to the British Fort Miami (present-day Fort Wayne, Indiana). First, the captured Americans were stripped of their clothes and possessions. Then the pestering turned deadly. Several prisoners were murdered. It was beginning to look like the River Raisin. This time, Tecumseh was near. When he found out what was happening, he yelled at his warriors to stop. The terrified prisoners were left alone.

Meanwhile, Proctor and his men had stayed outside Fort Meigs. Tecumseh returned from Fort Miami. He wanted Proctor to make a second attack. Tecumseh had a plan. He knew the Americans had sent for more reinforcements. The British and native warriors would trick the Americans. They would make the Americans believe these reinforcements had arrived and were being attacked. The warriors and the British soldiers moved out of sight of the fort. They yelled, screamed, and fired their muskets. Tecumseh thought the Americans would leave the fort to help their reinforcements. When they did, they would get a nasty surprise.

The trick almost worked. The men in the fort heard

the sounds of a pitched battle. They wanted to help, but their commander held them back. He suspected a trick.

Tecumseh had had enough. He forced Proctor to abandon the attack. During the next few weeks, Proctor and Tecumseh suffered many defeats. Dozens of Tecumseh's men left him. A British victory — and Tecumseh's dreams — seemed to be slipping away.

On September 10, 1813, British and American battleships waged a battle on Lake Erie. Proctor and Tecumseh watched from Fort Amherstberg. The British suffered their first naval defeat. Proctor was scared of losing the native alliance. He lied to Tecumseh. He tried to tell him that the British had won the battle.

Tecumseh was no fool. He knew the British had been defeated. He suspected they were planning to retreat. Tecumseh refused to run from his old enemy Harrison. He had no faith in Proctor. Instead, he turned to Matthew Elliot, the Indian Department representative. Tecumseh threatened Elliot. If Proctor retreated, he and his warriors would turn on the British and cut them to pieces. His threat was taken seriously. Tecumseh's warriors outnumbered the British regulars three to one.

On September 18, Elliot held a meeting between Tecumseh, Proctor, and the military advisors. Tecumseh accused the British of breaking their promise. He said they had abandoned his people. He reminded the assembly that they had not yet seen an American soldier in Amherstberg. They had not been defeated on

Canadian soil. Proctor then made his case for retreat. He promised the British would meet the enemy at a planned location along the Thames Valley. This would draw the Americans toward the east. They would be deep into Canadian territory. It would put them farther from reinforcements and supplies.

Tecumseh called Proctor a "miserable old squaw.' He accused the British of being "a fat animal that acts proud but drops its tail between its legs when challenged." His words did not work. The decision to retreat was made.

Tecumseh was trapped in his alliance with Proctor. He had no choice but to follow the retreat. He told his warriors, "We are going to follow the British, but I fear I will never return."

Proctor led the retreat. Within a few days, the British had left all of the Michigan Territory captured by Brock the year before. Half of Tecumseh's warriors deserted during the retreat.

The Storm

At last, Proctor stopped the retreat at a native village called Moraviantown (near present-day Chatham). Tecumseh and the warriors scouted behind the troops. They acted as a rear guard. Tecumseh did what he could to slow down the Americans. He destroyed a bridge. Then he started a fight with American scouts. It did not slow Harrison's troops for long.

That evening, Tecumseh stopped at a mill. He

waited for some of his warriors to catch up to him. Christopher Arnold was the settler who owned the mill. He was terrified. A band of native warriors had burned his neighbour's mill a few days before. He thought he was in for the same treatment. Tecumseh knew that his warriors had been told to burn everything that might be of use to the Americans. He also realized the settlers might not survive the winter without the mill. He stayed the night to protect the mill from his own men.

The next morning was October 5, 1813. Tecumseh asked Arnold to watch for American scouts. Meanwhile, he would wait in the woods. At the first sign of Americans, he was ready to gallop off to warn the British. He told the miller to pretend he was digging. As soon as he saw the scouts, he was to throw up a shovel of earth. Arnold agreed. Tecumseh's sharp eyes found the scouts first. He was gone before Arnold could give him the signal.

On his way to join Proctor, Tecumseh performed another kind act. Arnold had told him that his brother-in-law's family had no food. The miller had wanted to take them some flour. However, he was afraid to venture out. On his way to join the troops, Tecumseh rode by the brother-in-law's house. He tossed a bag of flour at the front door.

Tecumseh reached the troops. He began to prepare for combat. He was still eager to fight, but he worried about the coming battle. Proctor had not talked strategy with him. The troops had not eaten in days. They were low on ammunition, and they were greatly outnumbered. Proctor had barely 500 regulars and militiamen. Tecumseh now had only 500 warriors. Harrison commanded more than 3,000 well-armed Americans.

Tecumseh directed the battle. He positioned his warriors on the far edge of a great swamp. He placed Proctor and his men to the left. They would take their positions on some high ground between the Thames River and the swamp. He told the Canadian militia to take up a position between the two groups. Tecumseh warned Proctor to stand firm. Then he returned to the swamp to wait.

The American troops arrived at the battleground. The two armies faced each other for several hours. They were barely 275 metres apart. The Americans formed their lines. Finally, they were ready for combat. One battalion charged the British. A group of Kentucky militiamen advanced towards Tecumseh.

The Americans yelled, "Remember River Raisin," as they spurred their horses forward.

As Tecumseh had predicted, the horses got bogged down in the thick marsh. The Americans had to keep going on foot. Tecumseh's warriors cut them down.

However, the British line had broken. Proctor's soldiers were running for their lives. Tecumseh and his men had been abandoned. Harrison's troops closed in on the warriors. The warriors ran out of ammunition. They fought on with their tomahawks. Tecumseh's chilling war cry echoed through the forest. Then, there was only silence.

The great chief was never found. It is believed the warriors took his body with them when they retreated. There is no official record of Tecumseh's death. There is no official marker over his final resting place. To this day, the Shawnee elders say they know where he is buried. They say that the location of his grave has been passed down from one generation of leaders to the next.

Wherever Tecumseh lies, the hopes of a Native peoples' nation were buried with him. The grand alliance between the Native peoples and the British was finished. The last of the nations made peace with the Americans. The lands that Tecumseh had fought to keep free were sold to settlers. The Native peoples of Tecumseh's generation lived the rest of their lives on small parcels of reserved lands.

"The great barrier was broken," wrote one of his followers. "It was my last fight. My heart was big then. Tecumseh filled it. It has been empty ever since."

After the Battle of the Thames, Proctor was charged in military court for his actions. He lived out the rest of his days in disgrace. Brigadier General Harrison lacked enough supplies for the coming winter. He could not stay in Canada. He retreated back to Fort Detroit.

The war was at a stalemate once more. The borders were much the same as they had been in the early months of the war.

Chapter 4
1812–1814: Charles-Michel de Salaberry

In the spring of 1813, the Americans turned their attention from Upper Canada to Lower Canada. It was not as heavily defended as Upper Canada. They planned to capture Montreal. Then they could cut off the British supply line from the Atlantic. They discussed their plans in detail. Canadian spies were eavesdropping. They took the information back to a young lieutenant colonel in the British army. The officer was a French Canadian. His name was Charles-Michel d'Irumberry de Salaberry. He knew every move the Americans made.

De Salaberry was a soldier by choice and by tradition. For centuries, his family had served in armies

Charles-Michel de Salaberry

under the kings of France. In the 1700s, one of his ancestors moved the family to Upper Canada (then called New France). There, the de Salaberrys kept up the military tradition. The British defeated the French in Lower Canada in 1759. After that, part of the family returned to France. Those who stayed gave their loyalty to the French in Canada and to the British. Charles' father worked for the British administration. It was natural that the family would support the British against the Americans in the war of 1812.

Charles de Salaberry was born in Beauport, Lower Canada, in 1778. He joined the British army at age 14. He served in the West Indies. Then he fought Napoleon in Holland. His mentor and sponsor in the military was the Duke of Kent, father of the future Queen Victoria. The Duke was a close friend of Charles' father.

De Salaberry had a promising military career in England. Still, he wanted to return to Canada and his family. He was finally transferred home in the spring of 1812, just before the war began.

De Salaberry was 34 when he returned from England. He was a seasoned soldier and a man to be feared. It was his personality that people remembered. Honour meant more than life to de Salaberry. This was to be expected of a man with his background. A scar on his forehead was proof of that. While he was in Europe, a Prussian officer had bragged about killing a French Canadian. De Salaberry had told the Prussian to follow him outside. There, he could try to kill another. After the duel, only de Salaberry walked away.

The French Canadians were the wild card in the British deck of support. No one was really sure which side they would be on in the coming conflict. The Americans were counting on the French Canadians to support them. They believed the French Canadians were looking for a chance to overthrow the British. They were wrong. Most French Canadians did not like or trust American-style democracy. They wanted to protect their religion, culture, and language. The British promised these would be protected. French Canadians supported the British. However, they deeply resented being forced to serve in the militia.

In July 1812, the British sent Governor General George Prevost to Montreal. Prevost was to announce that 2,000 bachelors were being forced to serve in the militia. The French Canadians rose up in protest. There was a riot in the village of Lachine. The British rushed in. By the time they restored order, hundreds of men had been arrested. Two civilians had been killed. Prevost promised to pardon all the rioters. He also promised to protect French cultural rights in the militia.

The Voltigeurs

Prevost asked de Salaberry to recruit and train a French-Canadian militia unit. The unit would be called the *Voltigeurs*. (This word means "horseman," but de Salaberry's Voltigeurs didn't use horses.)

De Salaberry gathered the toughest men he could find. They had all been fur traders, trappers, and adventurers. De Salaberry drilled them all the time. They developed into one of Canada's best fighting units. They were as comfortable in the woods as they were on the battlefield.

De Salaberry recruited most of the officers from among his friends and members of his extended family. This didn't earn them any favours. De Salaberry may have attended their balls and family parties, however, he was a very serious soldier. He would allow no disrespect. No one was allowed to challenge his authority.

De Salaberry quickly earned the respect of his men. Early in their training, some men complained that de Salaberry was impossible to please. Later, they became his most loyal admirers. His rigid training made them into a confident fighting force. Their loyalty to the unit grew. This loyalty was tied directly to their commander.

The Voltigeurs knew that de Salaberry could scare them. Therefore, he should be able to strike terror into the hearts of their enemies. In late November 1812, two of de Salaberry's spies came to him with news. David and Jacob Manning told him that a large force of American troops was advancing towards the Canadian border. Their target was Montreal.

De Salaberry was confident in the 500 Voltigeurs and native warriors he commanded. In fact, he was so confident that he did not inform his superiors that the Americans were on the way. He believed that his men could easily hold off the much larger American force.

De Salaberry led his men to La Colle. It was a small village on the Canadian side of the Richelieu River, just north of Lake Champlain. De Salaberry knew that La Colle was the most likely entry point for the American force. He was right. In the early hours of November 27, 1812, an advance guard of about 800 American soldiers crossed La Colle Creek. De Salaberry and his men were waiting for them in a mill.

The Voltigeurs and their Mohawk allies were badly outnumbered. They held off the Americans for as long as they could. Finally, they retreated into the surrounding forest. It was not yet dawn. The Americans took possession of the mill. They prepared to pursue the Voltigeurs. Before they could, they were attacked again. The Americans fought furiously. When dawn broke, they learned the truth. In the darkness and confusion, they had been fighting another unit of their own militia. It was a unit that had crossed the creek just hours after they had.

De Salaberry launched a counterattack. The Americans were upset by the recent battle with their own comrades. They were too shaken to fight. They retreated back across the border. It was 12 months before they attempted another invasion of Lower Canada.

De Salaberry continued to recruit and drill his men. By the summer of 1813, he had recruited enough Voltigeurs to spare some. He sent about 500 men to help fight the Americans on the Niagara Peninsula. De Salaberry and his men also helped protect a British flotilla on Lake Champlain that summer. They provided cover while the flotilla harassed the Americans.

In the fall of 1813, the Americans were preparing to take Montreal again. Once more, the British and Canadians had to trick the Americans. They had to fool them into believing they had huge armies. Salaberry did this by marching his Voltigeurs from town to town and back again. His men complained, but he made them do it anyway.

The Battle of Chateauguay

In late September, the Americans began moving their troops into Lower Canada. This time, they had a different strategy. They planned a two-pronged attack on Montreal. One army would march along the banks of the Chateauguay River. A second, larger force would make its way up the St. Lawrence River by boat. The two rivers run parallel to each other. The Chateauguay runs slightly to the south. It joins the St. Lawrence a few kilometres south of Montreal. The two armies would meet near Kahnawake, about 30 kilometres south of Montreal. Then they would attack the city. The invasion force was huge. There were more than 10,000 soldiers.

The first army was led by General Wade Hampton. He was to draw attention away from the main force. It was gathering at Sacket's Harbour, New York. There, it would prepare to sail up the St. Lawrence. Hampton's troops headed towards the Canadian border.

David Manning was spying on them. He counted the guns, wagons, and soldiers. Manning had more than numbers to report to de Salaberry. To everyone's surprise, 1,400 New York militiamen refused to cross the border into Canada. By U.S. law, militiamen could not be forced to fight on foreign soil. The units from the northern states did not want to fight people they thought of as neighbours and friends. They also didn't want to be outside fighting during winter.

Some militiamen decided to stay with their general. Many were from the southern states. They lacked warm clothes. They were not prepared to face a harsh Canadian winter. Manning also reported on the other American force that was heading up the St. Lawrence under the command of Major General James Wilkinson. De Salaberry was thrilled with this information.

Hampton was furious about the loss of so many of his militia. Still, he felt confident about the coming attack. After all, he still had more than 4,000 men with him. On September 21, he created a diversion at Odelltown. The town lay just inside the Canadian border. The Americans surprised the small group of British soldiers stationed there. They killed three and captured six.

De Salaberry knew the Americans had crossed into Canada. The force he commanded was far too small to launch an attack. The best he could do was keep the Americans contained inside Odelltown. He sent out small units of Mohawks to cut off the American patrols. The Americans feared meetings with the native warriors. They stayed inside the town. Thus, they had no idea how small de Salaberry's force really was. The believed they faced a long, tough fight. They were also short of water. Once again, Hampton retreated back across his own border.

Right away, de Salaberry led his men on a forced 24-hour march to the Chateauguay Valley. He knew Hampton would return and take his troops along this valley. The Canadian wanted to be there to greet him. De Salaberry left soldiers along the way to serve as communication outposts. They would warn him when the Americans arrived. He finally reached the valley. There, he set up camp and waited for the Americans.

Meanwhile, the Americans had set up camp at Four Corners. It was a small town just inside the American border at the southern end of the Chateauguay Valley. This was about 15 kilometres from de Salaberry's camp. De Salaberry sent a few units of warriors and Voltigeurs to fire at the American camp. They terrorized the camp every night for two weeks. The Americans were so alarmed that they would not go outside their camp at night.

On October 1, de Salaberry received orders from Prevost. They were to raid the American camp. It seemed like a suicide mission. De Salaberry had several hundred Voltigeurs and warriors. Hampton had several thousand militiamen. De Salaberry had little hope of winning. De Salaberry later wrote to his father that he suspected Prevost was trying to get rid of him. In spite of this, de Salaberry followed orders and stormed the camp.

The Americans quickly recovered from their surprise. They launched a huge counterattack. During this attack, the Mohawks withdrew twice. Both times, de Salaberry brought them back. On the third withdrawal, they were gone for good. They took a number of Voltigeurs with them. Only de Salaberry and four of his men were left to fend off the Americans. When night fell, the five exhausted men were able to slip away. More attacks were out of the question.

De Salaberry returned to his camp. He knew that Hampton's plans had not changed. He and his men would soon be marching along the banks of the Chateauguay River. At Kahnawake, they would join up with the other invading force. De Salaberry took his men along the same route. He ordered them to destroy bridges. He made them chop down trees to scatter across the path behind them.

De Salaberry was determined. He would not allow Hampton to reach Kahnawake. He searched for a place to make a stand against the huge force. He chose a series of sharp ravines. The thick bush, blocked roads, and burned bridges slowed Hampton's troops. This gave de Salaberry the time he needed to prepare. His men fortified the ravines with an ***abatis***. Felled trees were piled atop one another with their tops pointing downwards.

In the meantime, Prevost realized that Montreal was the Americans' main target. He made plans to take reinforcements to de Salaberry by land. Then he sent for Lieutenant Colonel "Red George" Macdonell. (He was named Red George for his flaming red hair.) He asked Macdonell to take a battalion to de Salaberry by boat. Prevost asked Red George when he and his men could leave.

The lieutenant replied, "Right after we finish supper."

Red George reached de Salaberry on October 24. It was barely 60 hours since he had received his orders. He and his soldiers had travelled over 200 kilometres on the St. Lawrence River. De Salaberry was happy to see the reinforcements. Still, he knew the extra numbers would not ensure victory. They were still outnumbered three to one. It was time to try another bluff.

By this time, Hampton's troops were very close. They were close enough to see what they thought were hundreds of reinforcements marching towards de Salaberry's camp. De Salaberry had used Brock's trick. He had the same men march back and forth wearing what looked like different uniforms each time. They didn't have different uniforms. The men had just turned their jackets inside out.

Hampton was fooled. He believed de Salaberry's force was twice the size of his own. He gave up on the idea of a head-on assault. Instead, he sent a force of 1,500 men into the forests to attack de Salaberry's men. The Voltigeur scouts detected them. Red George and his men, along with a group of Voltigeurs, fought the Americans off.

That afternoon, Hampton decided to try a head-on

assault after all. The American troops advanced toward the ravines. De Salaberry fired the first shot. There was a furious exchange of fire. De Salaberry ordered his men to take cover behind the abatis. The Americans thought the Canadians and British were retreating. They began to cheer.

De Salaberry encouraged his men to return the victory shouts. These shouts came from the top of every ravine. Then Red George's men picked up the shouts from their reserve position in the woods. The Mohawks added to the ruckus with their war whoops. The Americans stopped cheering. They fired volley after volley into the woods at what they believed to be thousands of warriors. Finally, de Salaberry sent his buglers into the woods. They were to sound an imaginary advance.

Silence fell over both armies. De Salaberry called out to one of his Voltigeurs in French. He warned him to communicate only in French. He did not want the enemy to understand. The man replied that the Americans who had attacked them that morning had regrouped. They were attacking again. De Salaberry told him to draw the fight to the riverbank. When the Americans reached the river, they were met by the Voltigeurs. They fled back into the forest.

Hampton was outsmarted by his enemy once more. He ordered a general retreat. The dead and wounded Americans were left in the ravines. De Salaberry had the American wounded taken to a nearby field hospital, along with his own wounded.

Following the American retreat, de Salaberry's men set to work repairing the battlements. They thought the Americans would be back. De Salaberry expected only to gain some time with his bluffs. He didn't realize that he had won a complete victory against the Americans.

De Salaberry and his men spent the next eight days huddled against the abatis. A storm raged around them. They waited for an enemy who never returned. The men were miserable. One of the Voltigeurs wrote, "We suffered so much from … foul weather that some of our men fell sick every day. I now know that a man could endure without dying more pain and hell than a dog. There were many things that I could tell you easier than I could write them, but you would be convinced by this affair that Canadians know how to fight."

The Battle of Chrysler's Farm

The other arm of the American invasion force was 7,000 men strong. It was making its way up the St. Lawrence River in hundreds of light river boats. The flotilla made slow progress. From the Canadian side of the river, they were bombarded by cannon fire. Their commander, General Wilkinson, was sick. The soldiers were not in a hurry to go anywhere. It took them eight days to cover 130 kilometres.

Along the way, the American flotilla stopped to

question Canadian farmers. They hoped to get information about the British and Canadian forces. They also looted. This earned them the hatred of the locals. The Canadians told the Americans a series of outrageous lies. The rapids ahead were the size of Niagara Falls. The British and Canadian army was so large they couldn't count its numbers. This time, it was the civilians who tricked the Americans into believing they were up against a huge army.

Finally, on November 11, 1813, the American force reached a farm owned by a man named John Chrysler. (It was near the present-day town of Long Sault, Ontario.) They had to disable the cannons that were still firing at them from the Canadian side of the river. Then they would be able to keep going by boat. The dangerous Long Sault rapids were ahead. They could not get through them while under fire.

The Canadians and British had expected the Americans to stop at Chrysler's farm. They told the Chrysler family to hide in their cellar. Then they set up their troops in the surrounding fields. There were units of British regulars, native warriors, and the Voltigeurs. (De Salaberry had finally realized there would be no more action on the Chateauguay. He had led his men to the next battle.)

As always, the defending army was greatly outnumbered. They scattered in small groups. A unit of Voltigeurs hid in the woods. A band of Mohawks took a position in the cornfield. The British regulars waited beyond the barns. Everywhere the Americans looked, they could see the enemy.

The Americans had already received word of Hampton's defeat. His troops would not be joining the attack on Montreal after all. When they saw the troops at Chrysler's farm, they realized they would have to engage them. Wilkinson was still too ill to leave his bed. He ordered his junior officer to engage the British in the usual way. He would fight first one unit and then the next.

The officer followed his orders. It was a disaster. Just as the Americans appeared to defeat one unit of the enemy, another stood up to engage. At last, Wilkinson called the retreat. The tired soldiers piled into their boats. They retreated across the river to the American side. The attack on Montreal was over before it had begun.

Prevost tried to take credit for the Chateauguay victory. He had not arrived until the battle was all but over. In his official messages, he barely mentioned de Salaberry and the Voltigeurs. All he wrote was that they had served as the advance force for the British.

There were many witnesses to the Battle of Chateauguay. They wanted the truth to be known. De Salaberry was angry and sent his own accounts of the battle back to the high command in Britain. Accurate accounts of the battle also appeared in the *Montreal Gazette.*

The high command was not fooled by Prevost's claims. The legislature in Lower Canada congratulated de Salaberry on his victory. A representative of the Prince Regent made special mention of de Salaberry and the Voltigeurs in his remarks about the battle.

De Salaberry was too busy to bother himself much over Prevost's stories. His men were exhausted. They had been on the move since early September. They needed some rest.

Late in November, Prevost gave de Salaberry orders. He and his Voltigeurs were to stage a raid on an American camp at Four Corners, New York. This was the same camp where they had almost been destroyed two months before.

It seemed like a waste of time. Still, de Salaberry did his duty. He led 300 of his men back to Four Corners. It was cold and raining. They spent a miserable night in a makeshift camp. In the morning, the men awoke covered in frost. They also awoke to the news that one of their scouts was missing. They believed he had been captured by the enemy camp. But the scout returned. He reported that a large number of Americans were waiting for them with heavy gun support. De Salaberry knew when to quit. He withdrew.

De Salaberry suffered from rheumatism and fevers from his long military service. He thought about retirement. In January 1814, he received orders to head off a possible American attack on Coteau du Lac. He quickly called up 600 Voltigeurs and some of the 49th Regiment. They marched the 60 kilometres to Coteau du Lac. Two dozen men were lost to frostbite along the way. When they got there, they realized it was a false alarm. There were no Americans, and no attack about to happen. De Salaberry returned to Montreal in February. He was ill and disheartened.

He accepted a transfer that would take him out of direct fighting. However, the Americans returned. Together, he and his Voltigeurs defeated this last invasion force.

By that time, de Salaberry had had enough of military service. He had been at war for more than half of his life. He sent an official letter to the Duke of Kent. In his letter, he requested leave to retire. A peace was being discussed. The duke felt the war would soon be over. Could de Salaberry hold out for a few more months? Then he would be able to retire with the half-pay that was due to all officers who served the entire length of the war. De Salaberry stayed.

Charles-Michel de Salaberry received praise from his men, his generals, and his country. In 1818, he was appointed to the legislative council of Lower Canada. Years later, he was made a Companion of the Order of Bath.

Chapter 5
1812–1814: William Hamilton Merritt

William Hamilton Merritt was in most of the major battles of the War of 1812. He served as a militiaman in his father's unit. Later, he led his own troop of dragoons. William's father had fought for the British in the American War of Independence. After the war, he moved to Canada as a United Empire Loyalist. William thought of himself as a Canadian.

He had been born in Twelve Mile Creek. It was a small community at the northern end of the Niagara Peninsula. It was about 20 kilometres west of Fort George and the American border. The Niagara Peninsula was his home. He would fight to protect it.

The Horrors of War
By the age of 20, William Merritt had already fought

alongside Brock at Queenston. He had also fought with Fitzgibbon at Stoney Creek and Beaver Dams.

People were getting sick of war. They had lived in a war zone for many months. On July 8, 1813, Merritt took part in a violent battle between the Mohawks and Americans. Fighting with the Mohawks was a 13-year-old boy named John Lawe. His older brother had been killed in an earlier battle. His father had been wounded and taken prisoner. The boy wanted revenge. The battle was over. Still, the boy stumbled around the field. He was looking for the enemy. His mother came to find him. She carried the tired boy home in her arms.

Merritt was disgusted with the British whenever they retreated from the Niagara Peninsula. He felt they were abandoning the settlers on the frontier. Especially, they were walking out on the Loyalists. They would pay the biggest price when the Americans swarmed over the border. Like Fitzgibbon, Merritt was angry about the way the enemy harassed civilians. He swore to do something about it. Merritt and his fellow Dragoons galloped around the countryside, harassing the enemy. They did this even during the times when the militia had been disbanded. They clashed often with the hated raider Cyrenius Chapin and his guerrillas.

Merritt was angry with the Americans. However, it was the actions of a fellow Canadian that angered him the most.

The Hunt for a Traitor

Joseph Willcocks hated the British and anyone who sided with them. He had fought with Brock at Queenston. Since then, he had changed sides. He was the publisher of the *Upper Canadian Guardian*. He regularly attacked the British and Loyalists in print. He was jailed twice for libel. He was also elected to the government of Upper Canada.

Willcocks believed the Americans would win the war. In 1813, he turned on the people who had elected him. He started by spying for the Americans. Then he joined their army and became an officer. He also convinced more than 100 of his fellow Canadians to fight against the Canadians and the British.

In the fall of 1813, the Americans invaded the Niagara Peninsula again. By December, they had taken Fort George. They were also in Queenston and Chippewa. Willcocks and his men burned farms and arrested many Canadian men. At Twelve Mile Creek, Willcocks arrested an 80-year-old man. He was a former town warden and retired militiaman. The man was Thomas Merritt, William Merritt's father.

The Americans took Thomas across the border. They released him soon after. However, they left the old man to find his own way home. William Merritt was furious. He wanted to destroy the traitor Willcocks.

On November 28, 1813, Willcocks and his men were in the area of Twelve Mile Creek. William Merritt was close behind. Willcocks slipped away. However, two of Willcocks' men found Merritt and his men. They thought Merritt and his men were Americans. The blue uniforms the Canadians wore looked like the American uniforms. From these men, Merritt learned that Willcocks was headed for Burlington Heights. The American army was close behind. They were planning to attack the British there.

Merritt chased after the traitor. He came close, but Willcocks escaped. Willcocks told his superiors that the British force was much larger than it was. If the Americans thought the British force was huge, they would allow him to arrest more Canadians. Willcocks' information scared off the Americans. They abandoned their attack. They began marching back to Fort George.

Merritt and his commander, Colonel Murray, wanted to pursue the Americans. Both men believed they could defeat the Americans. They just had to get them outside the fort. However, they were under strict orders not to follow the retreating Americans beyond Twelve Mile Creek. It was a bitter blow.

Merritt was also very worried about his father. He found out that Thomas had reached Shipman's Corners between the British and American positions. Merritt asked for permission to leave Twelve Mile Creek. He said he was going to look for American spies. Instead, he went to bring his father home.

During his journey, he saw many American scouts.

He thought they were probably trying to count the size of the British force. When he got back to Twelve Mile Creek, he told the militia to gather in the town centre. Every available man and boy answered the call. The American scouts saw the huge crowd. They were convinced it was an advance party. They thought the entire British and Canadian force would soon follow. Of course, they wouldn't. The British had no intention of leaving Burlington Heights. However, Merritt's trick was enough. Brigadier General George McClure was the commander of Fort George. He decided to abandon the fort.

McClure made plans to withdraw across the Niagara River. He wanted to get to the safety of the American Fort Niagara. Willcocks was angry. He thought he had chosen the winning side. Now the Americans seemed to be abandoning their invasion of Canada.

The Americans decided to destroy Fort George. They didn't want the British and Canadians to use the fort. Willcocks asked McClure for permission to burn the nearby town of Newark before they burned the fort. He said this would stop the townspeople from offering shelter or supplies to British soldiers.

Newark on Fire!
At dusk on December 10, 1813, Willcocks and his men rode into the town of Newark. The townspeople were warned to take what they could from their homes and leave. It had been snowing all day. It was bitterly cold.

Willcocks started the burn at the home of William Dickson. He knew Dickson from his days in the government. He had arrested and imprisoned Dickson months before. Willcocks carried the firebrand himself. He went upstairs to find the elderly Mrs. Dickson in bed. She was too ill to walk. He ordered two of his men to carry her outside. The men wrapped the old woman in blankets. They left her in a snowdrift. She could only watch as Willcocks burned her home to the ground.

There were other horrible stories from that night. One young widow with three small children was turned out of her home with nothing but a few coins. After Willcocks' men burned her home, they took her money as well. In all, 400 women, children, and elderly men were turned out into the snow that night.

Merritt had been on an assignment in Beaver Dams that day with Colonel Murray. As they were on their way back home, they saw the orange glow of the fires in Newark. They guessed what had happened, and they raced to the scene. They were too late.

Merritt had seen a lot during the war. This was the worst. All that was left of Newark were glowing embers and charred buildings. There had been 150 homes in the town. Only one remained standing. The townspeople had crowded into every room until the house could hold no more. Those left outside huddled in the drifts and beneath makeshift shelters. Some were worried that there would be more attacks. They had stumbled off into the freezing night to seek shelter at outlying farms. Many wouldn't make it.

The streets were scattered with furniture, clothing, dishes, and personal treasures. The people were cold and too frightened to carry them. Nearly 100 townsfolk died that night in Newark.

Willcocks had his revenge. Soldiers and civilians were horrified. One good thing came out of it. The burning of Newark united the Canadian and British troops and the civilians.

Vengeance for Newark

Merritt was enraged. He was not alone. The British and Canadian troops swore revenge. Colonel Murray was furious. He ordered his troops to Fort George that very night. He ignored the direct orders of General Vincent not to advance.

British and Canadian troops galloped towards the fort. Willcocks and most of the American troops were already across the border. Colonel Murray and his men captured the few remaining Americans who were still at Fort George. Murray's superiors forgave him for ignoring their orders. The tragedy of Newark was just too great.

It wasn't over. Ten days later, Merritt and his Dragoons gathered all the boats they could find. They planned to follow the Americans across the icy river and attack them at Fort Niagara. It took several days and nights in the bitter cold to find all the boats they needed. Merritt was exhausted and feverish. He was unable to take part in the invasion.

The American fort was heavily defended and no easy target. However, it faltered quickly under the angry Canadian and British assault. The officers had a difficult time controlling their men. No one could forget Newark.

Within days, the American side of the Niagara River, from Fort Niagara to Buffalo, New York, was a charred ruin. When the raid was over, only three buildings were left standing in the town of Buffalo. American families lost their homes and possessions. Some lost their lives to native tomahawks. The war had taken a very ugly turn.

The Americans did not blame the British, the Canadians, or even the native warriors. They blamed George McClure. He had allowed the burning of Newark. He was taunted and threatened on the streets of Buffalo. Then his command was taken from him.

The winter of 1813 saw many horrors. Finally, it was too cold to fight any longer. The British and Canadian soldiers retreated to their side of the Niagara River to wait for the spring thaw.

The next move was from the Americans. They needed a victory. On July 3, 1814, they captured Fort Erie. Then they marched towards Fort Chippewa, 10 kilometres to the north. They reached it the next day. While the troops were marching, Merritt was having dinner with his parents at Twelve Mile Creek. He had just turned 21, and they were celebrating. As soon as he heard the news, Merritt raced to join the battle.

The next day, Major General Phineas Riall watched the Americans approach. He was the British commander at Fort Chippewa. The American soldiers were wearing grey uniforms. The militia wore this colour. Riall thought he was facing a unit of new militia recruits. He ordered a full frontal assault. He thought the militia would turn tail and run. These soldiers did not run. Riall and his men were facing an entire army of well-trained career soldiers. The Americans had run out of the blue wool used to make uniforms for the regular troops. They had used the grey instead.

The British retreated to the village. There, their cannons were in place. Reinforcements finally arrived. The Americans decided not to chase Riall's army. That night, the houses of Chippewa were filled with wounded and dying soldiers. It was a night the villagers would never forget.

Neither the British nor the Canadians were willing to give up the field. The British and Canadians withdrew to Fort George. The Americans camped on Queenston Heights. They waited for reinforcements to arrive by ship. However, the commander of the reinforcements was sick. He wouldn't let his ships sail without him. It was a long wait.

William Merritt spent most of the next month fighting small battles against the Americans. The Canadian people were once again in the battlefield. Willcocks and his band of traitors were riding again. They raided village after village. They plundered and forced the people to flee to the safety of the British forts.

Willcocks' men were not the only ones raiding. A small group of American soldiers were sick of waiting. They rode to the village of St. David's. They drove back the few British soldiers guarding the villagers. The Americans looted and burned. When Merritt and his men arrived to help, 40 homes had already been destroyed. This time, the American commanders did something. The soldiers responsible were punished. They were sent back to the United States in disgrace.

Lundy's Lane

On July 23, 1814, the Americans received word about the reinforcements they had been waiting for. They would not be coming. The British and Canadians had been getting more reinforcements almost daily. The next day, the American commander retreated to Chippewa in order to re-supply his troops. From there, he planned to attack Burlington Heights. In the meantime, the British and Canadians had mobilized. They marched to Lundy's Lane.

On July 25, the American commander sent out a brigade of 1,200 men. They were to search Lundy's Lane for enemy troops. The brigade was led by Colonel Winfield Scott. Merritt was also there looking for

American soldiers. He and his men stopped for refreshments at a tavern. It was owned by a widow named Deborah Wilson. The widow Wilson was well known to both armies. She dished out both liquor and information to the patrons seated at her wooden tables. She didn't care if they were British, Canadian, or American.

Merritt and his men were just about to sit down. A scout rushed in to tell them the Americans were on their way. The Canadians raced outside and jumped on their horses. As the American brigade approached, they began firing. Merritt paused for a second. He cheekily waved to them before galloping off.

Scott searched the tavern, but no soldiers were found. Then he questioned the widow Wilson. She quickly told Scott what Merritt had told her. Major General Riall was waiting at a nearby farm with 1,100 men. The information was only partly right. Riall was nearby, but he had almost three times that many soldiers.

Scott was anxious to fight. He did not want to wait for reinforcements. Instead, he rushed in to engage the enemy. He had 1,200 men. The 1,100 men with Riall should not prove to be a problem.

The battle raged all afternoon and into the night. The two armies were often only metres apart. They could easily see the faces of their enemies. Still they fought on, firing volley after volley.

Joseph Willcocks was at the battle. He was afraid of being captured. He knew the Canadians would hang him as a traitor. He feared the Americans would lose. Around midnight, he disappeared into the darkness.

In the blackness of that night, horrible mistakes were made. Troops fired on themselves. Men engaged in hand-to-hand combat. Sometimes the men they fought with were their own men.

At one point, a group of American soldiers fought their way through the woods and surrounded Riall. He was taken prisoner, but his men fought on. William Merritt tried to rescue Riall. Merritt was also captured.

By morning, the men of both sides were too tired to keep going. The battle was finally over. The Americans quit the field. They left their wounded and heavy artillery behind. The British were in no condition to follow the retreating Americans. The battlefield was littered with hundreds of bodies. Some were just men who had fallen into an exhausted sleep in the middle of the battle. It took all morning to separate the wounded from the dead.

In their hasty retreat back to Fort Erie, the Americans had to dump wagonloads of supplies and arms. The wagons had to be used to transport the wounded. William Merritt was forced to take part in that retreat. The Americans took him and their other prisoners with them to jails in the United States.

Lundy's Lane was one of the bloodiest battles of the war. The British and Canadians suffered 880 men wounded, captured, or killed. The Americans suffered a similar number of casualties. Both sides claimed victory.

Whimpers of War

At the end of July, the Americans in Fort Erie were preparing for another invasion. Their plans were interrupted. On August 15, 1814, the British attacked the fort. The British and Canadians won an important victory at the battle. They finally drove the Americans back across the border. William Merritt's friends and family at Twelve Mile Creek had endured their last battle. So had the other Niagara villagers. They had also endured their last torment from Joseph Willcocks. The hated traitor had been killed at the battle. Merritt was imprisoned in the United States. He cheered when he heard the news.

On August 25, 1814, the Canadians and British swarmed into the naval base at Bladensburg, New York. They easily disarmed the militia guarding this entrance to Washington. By nightfall, the capital of the United States had been set on fire. Public buildings were looted. Documents littered the city streets.

In the Belgian town of Ghent, British and American politicians met to discuss the terms of peace. As they talked, soldiers kept fighting.

The Canadians and British won a series of naval victories on Lake Champlain. Both the Americans and the British were in a race to build bigger and better ships. The war with Napoleon was at an end. Recently, 16,000 battle-hardened troops had arrived in Canada to help end the war.

In September, Governor Prevost began a march

on Plattsburgh, New York. He led the largest army the British had fielded to date. His land attack was supposed to happen at the same time as a British naval attack on Plattsburgh Bay. However, Prevost was in a hurry. He put pressure on the naval commanders to engage. They were not ready, but they gave in and followed his commands. The battle was over in just over two hours. The British surrendered. It was the first time they had ever been defeated at sea.

Prevost's troops outnumbered the enemy three to one. Still, he called for a retreat. His commanders tried to argue with him. Prevost refused to listen. The army retreated. They were halfway to the Canadian border before the Americans even realized they were gone.

On January 8, 1815, British and Canadian troops attacked the port of New Orleans, Louisiana. The Americans won a stunning victory. The toll for the British and Americans was 2,000 dead or wounded.

Victory!

This victory might have won the war for the Americans. In fact, for a few weeks after the battle, the American people believed they had won. However, the battle had been fought for nothing. Two weeks before the battle, on December 24, 1814, the treaty had been signed in Ghent. It officially ended the war.

Word of the peace finally reached North America in February 1815. William Merritt was allowed to go back home to Twelve Mile Creek. He married and raised a family in the little town he loved. A few years later, he proposed the building of the Welland Canal. He also helped convince the American and Canadian governments to build a bridge across the Niagara River. It was the former border between the two countries.

Glossary

abatis: A barricade of trees with bent or sharpened branches directed toward the enemy.

advance party: A group of soldiers who go ahead of the main army to gather information and make certain that the road ahead is safe

Caughnawaga: A native American group that lived in and around the northeastern United States and north-eastern Canada

Dragoons: A type of soldier who could fight on foot or on horseback

legislature: An elected branch of the government with the power to make laws. There were legislatures in both Upper and Lower Canada.

militia: Citizens who were part-time soldiers. They only served as soldiers in emergencies.

Mohawk: A native American group that lived in and around the state of New York

mutiny: A rebellion against authority (e.g., soldiers rebelling against their superiors)

reinforcements: Additional soldiers called up to help

scouts: Soldiers who go on ahead of the main army to gather information

Shawnee: A native American group that lived in and around Ohio

The Canadas: The name originally given to Canada. At the time of the War of 1812, Canada was still a colony of Britain and not yet an independent country.

truce: A temporary end to fighting during a war

United Empire Loyalists: Men and women who remained loyal to Britain during the American War of Independence. Many fled to Canada when the Americans won their independence.

Wyandot: A native American group that lived in Ohio and the upper mid-western states

Bibliography

Berton, Pierre. *Flames Across the Border 1812-1813.* Toronto: McClelland and Stewart, 1981.

Berton, Pierre. *The Invasion of Canada 1812-1813.* Toronto: McClelland and Stewart, 1980.

Elliot, James. *Billy Green and the Battle of Stoney Creek, June 6, 1813.* Stoney Creek: Battlefield House Museum.

Hitsman, Mackay J. *The Incredible War of 1812: A Military History.* Toronto: Robert Brass Studio, 1999.

Mackenzie, Ruth. *James Fitzgibbon: Defender of Upper Canada.* Toronto: Dundurn Press, 1983.

Mackenzie, Ruth. *Laura Secord: The Legend and the Lady.* Toronto: McClelland and Stewart, 1971.

McLeod, Carol. *Legendary Canadian Women.* Nova Scotia: Lancelot Press, 1983.

Ryerson, Edgerton. *Loyalists of America and Their Times.* Toronto: 1880. The Historical Memorandum of Amelia Ryerse.

Stanley, George. *The War of 1812: Land Operations.* Toronto: Macmillan of Canada, 1983.

Sugden, John. *Tecumseh: A Life.* New York: H. Holt, 1998.

Sutherland, Stewart, Ed. *A desire of serving and defending my country: the War of 1812 journals of William Hamilton Merritt.* Toronto: Iser Publications, 2001.

Wohler, Patrick J. *Charles de Salaberry: Soldier of the Empire, Defender of Quebec.* Toronto: Dundurn Press, 1984.

Acknowledgments

I would like to recognize the National Archives of Canada, Pierre Berton's The Invasion of Canada and Flames Across the Border and Patrick Wohler's book on Charles de Salaberry as sources for the quotes used in this book.

Thank you to my editor, Pat Kozak, for her work and help.

I also want to thank my husband Alex and my history-loving daughters — Danielle, Kathleen, Alexandria, Emily, and Laura — for their unstinting support, and my parents, Terry and Linda Burke, for encouraging my own interest in history.

Finally, thank you to Ruth and Dan Crump for their interest and encouragement, and for the numerous tours of the areas known to Tecumseh and Brock as Forts Amherstberg and Detroit.

About the Author

Jennifer Crump is a freelance journalist and author whose work has appeared in numerous North American magazines, including *Reader's Digest, Canadian Geographic,* and *Today's Parent.* She is also the author of a guidebook on the city of Toronto. When she's not writing, she is reading. History, particularly Canadian history, is a long-time passion. A former resident of the southern part of Upper Canada, Jennifer now lives with her family in the northern part of the province.

Photo Credits